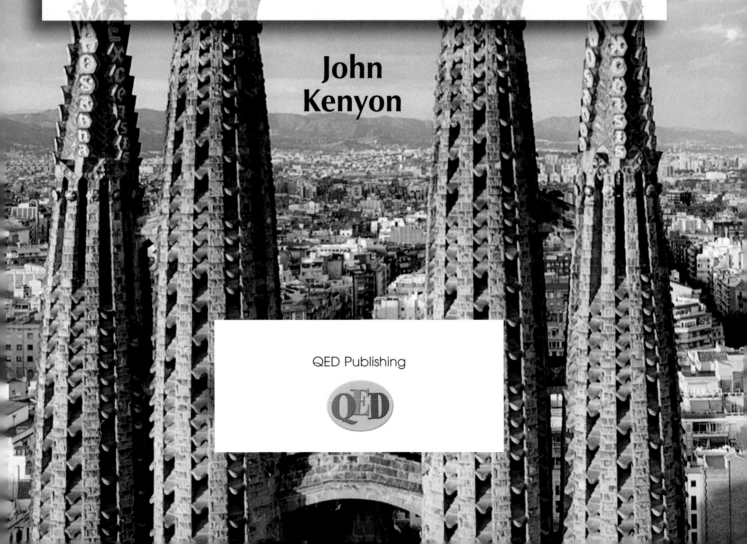

Spain

Come on a journey of discovery

John Kenyon

QED Publishing

QED

Copyright © QED Publishing 2004

First published in the UK in 2004 by
QED Publishing
A division of Quarto Publishing plc
The Fitzpatrick Building
188–194 York Way, London N7 9QP

A Catalogue record for this book is available from
the British Library.

ISBN 1 84538 061 4

Written by John Kenyon
Designed by Starry Dog Books Ltd
Editor Christine Harvey
Maps by PCGraphics (UK) Ltd

Creative Director Louise Morley
Editorial Manager Jean Coppendale

Picture credits

Key: t = top, b = bottom, m = middle, c = centre,
l = left, r = right

Corbis Krist J Black 12tr,/ Francesc Muntada 14–15,/
Jose Luis Palaez 15br,/ Attal Serge 18bl,/ Gunter Marx
19br,/ Reuters 20–21,/ Paul Almasy 21br,/ 26–27 Yann
Arthus-Bertrand,/ O Alamany and E Vicens 26bl, 27tr;
Spanish Tourist Board 3t,/ JJ Pascual Lobo 3m;
Getty Pete Adams 1,/ Robert Frerck 6m,/ James
Strachan 8–9,/ Ian Shaw 9br,/ Doug Armand 13tr,/
Gerard Loucel 22–23,/ Frank Herholdt 24br,/ Rudolf
Pigneter 24–25;
Art Directors and TRIP M Feeney 7m,/ H Rogers 8bl,
16–17, 22t,/ T Bognar 10–11,/ B Turner 10–11c, 19t,/ J
Dallet 12–13, 23tr,/ D Houghton 17tl,/ Viesti Collection
17tr.

Printed and bound in China

Words in **bold** can be
found in the Glossary
on page 28.

Contents

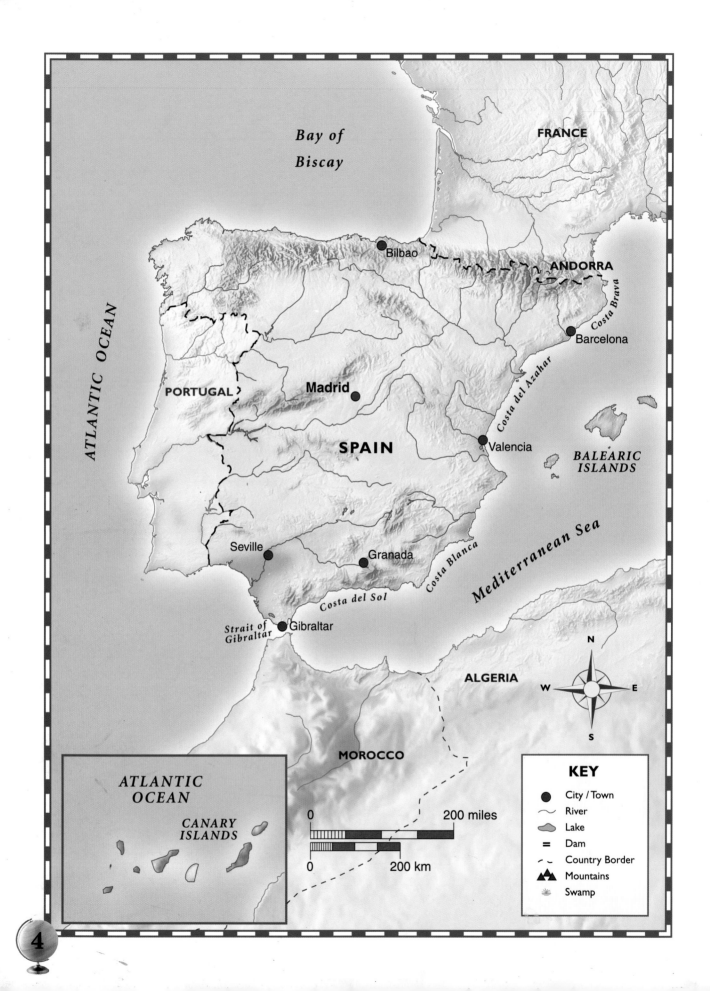

Bay of
Biscay

FRANCE

ATLANTIC OCEAN

Bilbao

ANDORRA

Costa Brava

Barcelona

PORTUGAL

Madrid

Costa del Azahar

SPAIN

Valencia

BALEARIC
ISLANDS

Seville

Granada

Costa Blanca

Mediterranean Sea

Costa del Sol

Strait of
Gibraltar

Gibraltar

ALGERIA

N

W   E

S

MOROCCO

ATLANTIC
OCEAN

CANARY
ISLANDS

0   200 miles

0   200 km

KEY

● City / Town
∼ River
Lake
= Dam
- - - Country Border
▲▲ Mountains
✳ Swamp

4

Where in the world is Spain?

Spain lies on the **continent** of Europe. It is part of a large **peninsula** called the Iberian Peninsula. Three countries border Spain. To the north is France, to the north east is Andorra and to the west is Portugal. At the southern tip is the British dependency of Gibraltar. The Canary Islands (located off the north west coast of Africa) and the Balearic Islands are also part of Spain.

Forty million people live in Spain. Spain has the fifth largest population of all the countries in Europe. Spain is about twice as large as the UK.

▼ Spain and its place in the world.

▲ The national flag of Spain.

Did you know?

Name Spain
Location South west Europe
Surrounding countries France, Portugal, Andorra and Gibraltar (dependency)
Surrounding seas and oceans Mediterranean Sea, Atlantic Ocean, Bay of Biscay
Length of coastline 4964km
Capital city Madrid
Area 504 782km^2
Population 40 217 413
Average life expectancy Male and female 79 years
Religion 94 per cent of the population is Roman Catholic
Languages Castilian Spanish is the official language
Climate Central Spain: hot summers and cold winters; northern coastal areas: mild climate; eastern and southern areas: warm wet winters and hot dry summers
Highest mountain range Sierra Nevada
Major rivers Tagus (length: 1007km), Ebro (length: 910km), Duero (length: 895km), Guadiana (length: 778km), Guadalquivir (length: 657km)
Currency Euro (previously pesetas)

What is Spain like?

▼ Traditional windmills are still used to make flour in the Meseta, the central plateau of Spain.

Spain's regions

The **mainland** of Spain is divided into 17 regions. Each region has its own capital city or town, and its own culture and traditions.

The north

The north east of Spain has a range of high mountains called the Pyrenees. They stretch for 450km. This mountain range marks the border between Spain and France.

The west

The northern and western **coasts** of Spain face the Atlantic Ocean. This coast has rocky **inlets** called *rias*.

The Meseta and central Spain

The largest area of Spain is on a **plateau** called the Meseta, which spreads for hundreds of kilometres from the middle of Spain. It covers 40 per cent of Spain's land. The capital city, Madrid, is situated in the very centre of the country.

Eastern and southern Spain

Spain has more than 2000 beaches. The majority are located to the east and south of Spain along the coast of the Mediterranean Sea. Millions of people come to these areas from other countries to enjoy holidays on the warm, sunny beaches. Barcelona, Spain's second largest city, is on the east coast.

▲ Spanish beaches, such as Benidorm, attract thousands of tourists every summer.

Climate

Spain has such a large land area that the climate varies a lot. If you travel through the whole country, you will notice that some parts of Spain are much warmer or cooler than others.

Francesca lives in Madrid. Her pen-friend in England has asked her to describe what the weather is like there.

In summer Madrid is really hot, especially at midday. School has a two-hour break in the afternoon and I go home for lunch. After lunch I usually keep cool by staying at home until it is time to go back to school. Sometimes, if it is not too hot, I go out and play with my friends.

In the winter it can be quite cold and I have to wrap up well when I'm walking to school or if I go out to visit a friend. And the church is often really chilly on Sunday mornings!

Central Spain

The central plateau of Spain is very hot in the summer and very cold in the winter. There is only a small amount of rainfall during the year.

Madrid can reach temperatures as high as 40°C in the summer and as low as -10°C in winter.

The Mediterranean coastline

The east and south east of Spain lie along the Mediterranean Sea coastline. These areas have hot summers and warm winters. The southern inland region of Andalusia is the hottest and driest part of Europe.

AVERAGE TEMPERATURES ACROSS SPAIN (°C)

Months	Jan	Feb	March	April	May	June	July	Aug	Sept	Oct	Nov	Dec
Bilbao (northern)	12	13	15	16	19	22	25	25	24	20	16	13
Seville (southern)	11	12	14	16	19	23	27	27	25	19	15	11
Madrid (central)	5	7	9	11	15	20	24	24	20	14	9	6

▲ The places mentioned in this chart are on the map on page 4.

▼ Because Madrid lies in the middle of Spain it has a very dry climate. The winters are fairly mild, but the nights can be freezing. The summers are hot, but the heat is dry and quite bearable.

Carlos lives in the eastern part of Spain, in Benidorm. He has written to his English pen-friend about the weather in his home town.

Benidorm is warm all the year round. It can be quite hot in the summer. In the winter it is cooler and this is when most of the rain falls. I prefer the autumn when there are not so many tourists and the beaches are not so crowded. Then I can play football on the beach with my friends!

Tom Collins
11 Apple Orchard
Somertown
Brightsea
ZZ5 8YR
UK

Mountains and rivers

Mountains in the north and south

Spain is a very mountainous country. The highest ranges are in the far north and south of the country.

The Pyrenees lie in the north, and the mountains in the south are called the Sierra Nevada. The Sierra Nevada mountains look down on the Mediterranean Sea holiday resorts. Both ranges have mountains that reach over 3400m above sea level.

Central Spain's mountains

The Meseta, Spain's central plateau, is surrounded by mountain ranges. Even though it can be very hot in the lowland plains of the Meseta, some of the higher mountain ranges are snow-capped. There are ski resorts in the Guadarrama mountains to the north west of Madrid.

▼ The snowy Pyrenees are a popular skiing destination.

Spain's main rivers

There are five main rivers in Spain. They all have their **source** in the mountain ranges in the Meseta. Four of the rivers flow westwards to the Atlantic Ocean. One of these, the Tagus, is the longest river in Spain. The fifth river, the Ebro, flows east to the Mediterranean Sea.

The River Guadalquivir

It is so hot in the Meseta that all the rivers can run dry in places. The most important river is the Guadalquivir, as it is used for river transportation and to **irrigate** farmland. The river flows through Seville, which is Spain's only port served by a river rather than the sea.

◄ Seville is located on the River Guadalquivir.

Did you know?

The highest mountain in mainland Spain is Mulhacen (3483m) in the Sierra Nevada.

The highest mountain in Spain is Pico de Teide, on the island of Tenerife (in the Canary Islands). It is 3718m high.

The Canary Islands lie 1500km off south west mainland Spain, directly opposite the coast of Morocco.

▼ This map shows Spain's mountain ranges and major rivers.

11

Getting around Spain

Travelling by air

Air travel is the fastest-growing form of transport in Spain. The country's increased popularity as a tourist centre has encouraged cheap air flights in and out of Spanish airports. There are airports near all the major cities in Spain.

Travelling by road

As Spain developed into an **industrialized** nation, it meant that a modern road system was important. Lorries and cars needed to be able to travel quickly between cities and towns. There is a system of modern main roads called *carretreras* and a motorway system known as *autopistas*. If you travel through Spain by car, you will have to pay a **toll** to use the motorways.

▲ Madrid has its own underground railway system so people can get around the city quickly.

Solving pollution

The increased traffic in towns and cities has caused worrying levels of air pollution. Cities such as Barcelona and Madrid have tried to reduce this problem by improving public transport, such as bus and train services. Many towns also have trams that run along the main roads.

Travelling by train

Spain has one of Europe's most technologically advanced railways, called the AVE. Introduced in 1992, it uses high-speed tilting trains that can travel at speeds up to 300km per hour. The high-speed train line connects Seville in the south of Spain with Madrid, and this journey takes only two and half hours. The same journey would take more than six hours by car.

▲ Traffic congestion in Madrid causes high levels of air pollution.

Amazing, but true!

The Romans built the first road system in Spain when they ruled there from 200 BC.

Spain has the highest road in Europe. It is in the Sierra Nevada in Andalusia and reaches 3496m.

Spain's major roads all start from Madrid in the centre of the country.

◄ The AVE is one of the fastest trains in the world.

Travelling around the regions of Spain

The history of the regions

Spain is made up of 17 separate regions. Originally these regions were small countries, but they were united in the 15th century under King John II and King Ferdinand of Aragon.

Many Spanish people like to identify themselves as citizens of a particular region, rather than of Spain.

Popular tourist regions

The regions of Catalonia, Valencia, Murcia and Andalusia are the areas that many tourists visit to enjoy the hot weather and beaches in the summer. Barcelona, the second largest city in Spain, is in Catalonia. Many of the old castles of Catalonia have been preserved and are popular tourist attractions.

▶ There are lots of beautiful buildings, such as Belmonte Castle, in Spain.

Madrid is in Castile Leon, which means 'land of the castle'. To the north east, the regions of Navarre and Aragon border France.

In the northern region of Spain, many of the people are fiercely independent and do not wish to be part of Spain. This area is known as the Basque country.

Languages

The official Spanish language is also called Castilian. The regions also keep alive their own traditional languages. The other main languages spoken are Catalan in Catalonia, Galician, which is spoken in Galicia in north west Spain, and Euskera (the Basque language) in the Basque country.

Anna lives in Valencia. She wrote in her diary about an unusual annual festival of the region.

Today was the tomato-throwing festival to celebrate the harvesting of the tomatoes in the region. We all had great fun running around the streets throwing tomatoes at each other! I got hit so many times that I was covered in tomato juice. It was even in my shoes!

Travelling through agricultural Spain

Farming

When you travel through some Spanish villages, you will still see the old, small-scale methods of farming. During the last 30 years, a lot of village farmers working the land have been replaced by businesses with advanced farming machinery.

The climate

The weather affects what can be grown in Spain. Travelling around the regions, you will see different crops growing, depending on the temperature and rainfall.

The north

The wet areas in the north of Spain are good for growing fruits, such as apples, pears, plums, melons and peaches. There are also large areas of **pastureland** for cattle, for the production of meat and milk.

◄ Spain produces a large quantity of onions, which it exports around the world.

▼ Spain is one of the world's largest producers of wine.

Central Spain

Irrigation makes some of the **arid** areas in this hot plateau more suitable for growing crops. Wheat and rice are the main crops here. Sheep and goats are also raised in this area.

The south and east

In the warm climate of the south and east, citrus fruits, grapes and olives can be easily grown.

▼ Many farms in Spain have their own windmills to supply power for pumping water.

Did you know?

Olives are one of Spain's most important crops and they are grown all over the country.

Grapes for making wine are grown in most regions of Spain.

Cork is one of Spain's major products. Cork comes from trees and is used for making bottle stoppers, floor coverings and pin boards.

The main crops grown on the Canary Islands are bananas and tomatoes.

Travelling through modern industrial Spain

Moving to the towns

Spain today is a modern industrial country. Over the last 40 years, many young people have left their villages in the countryside to go in search of work in the cities, where they can get higher wages. More than 90 per cent of Spain's population work in offices or factories.

As you travel around the Spanish countryside, you will notice that very few people live there.

The capital

Madrid is a large city with a population of more than three million people. The city has lots of manufacturing industries. Many people also have jobs in banking, business and the media (for example, newspapers and television).

▼ About two million cars are made in Spain each year.

▲ There are lots of interesting places in Madrid, like the Puerta de Europa office buildings.

Other industries

In the north of Spain, the main centre of industry is around the Basque region, where people work in mining and steel making. These older industries have started to be replaced by new technology industries, such as manufacturing electronics.

Around Barcelona there are a number of major industries, such as **textile** and car manufacturing.

For a school social history project, Francesca talked to her grandfather about how his life had changed since he was a boy.

My grandfather's name is Pedro. It was his 75th birthday last year. He lives in a small village near Seville in the region of Andalusia. Times have changed since he was a child. His father used to work on a farm that grew oranges. When the oranges ripened, my grandfather used to help pick them with his friends and he said they used to have fun juggling the oranges during the breaks! He misses the good old days when there were lots of people living in his village. Many of the young people have now left to work in the towns or at the tourist resorts. He says his village is much quieter these days.

Festivals and traditions

Fiestas in Spain

Spain is famous for its festivals called *fiestas*. There is usually a religious theme to a fiesta. The celebration will normally start with a church service.

There are important dates when all the people in Spain hold celebrations. The 25th of July is St James's day. St James is the patron saint of Spain so there are celebrations throughout the country.

Fiestas in the regions

Every region and town in Spain has holidays set aside for their own special fiestas. These fiestas often celebrate important people and events; for example, saints' days may be celebrated, or the successful harvesting of crops.

▶ Fiestas often include flamenco dancing, with men and women wearing colourful costumes.

▼ On special festival days, bulls are let loose in some village streets and people run along with them.

Bullfighting

Bullfighting is a popular type of entertainment in Spain. Some people believe bullfighting is cruel because the bulls are killed as part of the show. Others view bullfighting as an important part of Spanish culture. In Pamplona, in northern Spain, bulls are let loose in the streets during the Festival of San Fermin.

Traditional dancing

In southern Spain there is a traditional type of dance called *flamenco*. Dancers click the heels and toes of their shoes on the ground. The women wear colourful dresses and often hold small musical instruments called *castenets*. These are made of two curved discs of wood which are clicked together.

Miguel wrote a postcard to his British pen-friend about a fiesta in his region.

Dear Sam

Today is the 19th of March – St Joseph's day. In Valencia there is a fiesta for carpenters. This is because Joseph (who married Mary, the mother of Jesus) was a carpenter. Large statues are made from wood and wax, and prizes are given to the best ones. In the evening, bonfires are lit and the sky sparkles with fantastic firework displays.

Miguel

Sam Smith
34 Hedgeview Road
Townsfield
Watfordshire
XY13 2NJ
UK

▲ On St Joseph's Day, the streets of Valencia are richly decorated with flowers and oranges.

21

food and drink

► Tapas bars are very popular in Spain.

Spanish lunch

Traditionally, lunch was an important time for all the family to gather together. The Spanish lunch, *la comida*, took place between 2pm and 3pm. However, the fast pace of life in industrial towns has made family lunches less common. The traditional main meal, if it happens, can be as late as 11pm!

Tapas

Tapas is a popular type of food in Spain. It started as a small snack that was served in Spanish bars. It was provided as a light meal in the late morning to keep people going until lunch. Now tapas is served all day and tapas restaurants can be found all over the world.

Regional dishes

The different regions of Spain have their own special dishes. Andalusia is famous for its seafood, and also for a cold soup called *gazpacho*, which contains tomatoes and garlic. In Catalonia, a popular meal is *escalivada*, which is grilled vegetables, often served with grilled meat.

Wine

Spain is one of the largest wine producers in the world. The most famous wine from Spain is *Rioja*. Sherry is a strong wine that is unique to Spain. It takes its name from the area where it is produced – Jerez in Andalusia in southern Spain.

▼ In Spain, families like to get together at meal times.

▲ Paella is a rice dish containing different meats and seafood.

Juan lives in Barcelona. Read about the different meals he has during the day.

For breakfast I have bread and jam. School starts at 9.30am and finishes at 4.30pm. I have a two-hour lunch break so I go home and my mother makes a meal for me. My favourite is pasta in tomato sauce for the primero (first course) and for segundo (second course) I like paella. To finish I have fruit. My father works at the car factory and does not get home until 8pm. We wait for him to come home before we have our dinner. I like it best when we have tortilla with salad.

Tourism

How many tourists come to Spain?
More than 60 million people visit Spain each year. That is more people than actually live there!

Coastal attractions
Many people come to Spain to enjoy sunbathing on the beaches and swimming in the warm Mediterranean Sea. Coastal resorts stretch out along the eastern coastline from the Costa Brava in the north east to the Costa del Sol in the south east. Over the last 40 years this coastline has been developed. Hundreds of hotels, bars, nightclubs and shops have been built. The islands of Spain are also popular with many tourists.

▶ One of Spain's most famous churches is the Sagrada Familia in Barcelona.

Towns and cities
If you visit Spain, you may well spend time enjoying the towns and cities in the interior. There are many well-preserved castles and buildings for tourists to visit. Madrid has famous art galleries and museums. Barcelona is another popular city for foreign visitors. It has unusual buildings designed by an architect called Gaudí. Perhaps the most famous of his buildings is the Sagrada Familia church. This building is known as 'the sandcastle church' because of its shape.

The tourist industry

Many Spanish people have jobs that are created by the tourist trade. These jobs range from building hotels to working in them as waiters and cleaners. Tourism is the biggest industry for employment in Spain and has helped it become a richer and more modern European country.

▼ Many tourists enjoy the beaches on the Spanish Balearic island of Majorca.

Ben went to visit his Spanish pen-friend. He wrote a postcard to his Grandma during his stay.

Dear Gran
I'm having a great time in Benidorm. We went to the beach yesterday and swam in the sea. I made friends with some Spanish boys and they taught me a few Spanish words and phrases. I've found a nice present for you – a traditional Spanish basket.

Love from Ben

Granny Jones
11 Seaview Road
Northover
Southfield
AZ3 7YT
UK

Environmental issues

Spain's natural habitats

Spain has lots of wide open spaces that have not been developed for people to live in. This means that **habitats** for rare wild animals have not been disturbed. Wild brown bears, wolves and wild boars still live in the mountainous regions in the north of the country. In the warmer climates of the south there are also rare animals, especially reptiles, which are suited to the weather there.

National parks

The increase in **industrialization** has placed important rare animal and plant life in danger. The Spanish authorities are attempting to preserve habitats for animals and plants in a number of **national parks**.

There are ten large national parks in Spain. The three most important are:

• Donana National Park in southern Spain provides a protected area for many species of birds. The last surviving lynxes (a type of wild cat) in southern Europe also live here.

◀Wild lynxes are found in Donana National Park in southern Spain. They can grow to the size of a medium dog.

26

• Ordesa National Park is in the north, and includes part of the Pyrenees. The only herd of *ibex*, the Pyrenean mountain goat, in the world is found in this park.

• Montaña de Covadonga National Park in north west Spain provides habitats for rare birds such as the royal eagle. There are more than 40 types of orchid (a rare flower) in the area.

Coastal development

The building of hotels and tourist attractions along the Mediterranean coast has destroyed some important sandy areas and **wetlands**. The Spanish authorities have put stricter controls over building in these areas to protect the natural environment.

▼ In Spain's national parks the natural environment is protected from development.

Glossary

agriculture
farming land to produce food

arid
dry, with low rainfall

coast
where land meets the sea

continent
a large area of land. There are seven continents in the world: Africa, Asia, Australia, Antarctica, North America, South America, Europe

habitat
the natural home of a plant or animal

industrialized
area with many factories where a lot of manufacturing takes place

interior
the central part of a country, not near the coast

inlet
a narrow part of the sea that comes further into the land

irrigation
a method of storing and distributing water in order to grow crops

mainland
the main part of a country, not including its islands

national park
an area of land owned by the government where wild animals and plants are protected

pastureland
an area of land with grass on it, where cattle are kept

peninsula
a piece of land almost surrounded by water

plateau
a high flat area of land

source
where a river starts in a highland area

textile
cloth that is manufactured

toll
a cost that you must pay in order to use something; often a motorway

wetland
areas where the soil contains a lot of water

Index

Teaching ideas and activities for children

The following activities address and develop the geographical 'enquiry' approach, and promote thinking skills and creativity. The activities in section A have been devised to help children develop higher-order thinking, based on Bloom's taxonomy of thinking. The activities in section B have been devised to promote different types of learning styles, based on Howard Gardner's theory of multiple intelligences.

A: ACTIVITIES TO DEVELOP THINKING SKILLS
ACTIVITIES TO PROMOTE RESEARCH AND RECALL OF FACTS
Ask the children to:
• make an alphabet book for a young child, illustrating the contrasts in the regions of Spain.
• research and investigate a mountain environment (the Pyrenees or Sierra Nevada) or a coastal environment. The children could present their information in a poster or a Powerpoint presentation.

ACTIVITIES TO PROMOTE UNDERSTANDING
Ask the children to:
• use this book and other non-fiction books, CD-ROMs and the Internet to find out about tourism in Spain. They can use this information to write a script for a TV travel programme.
• use this book and other sources of information to find out about industries in Spain (such as car manufacturing, wine and sherry production or cork).

ACTIVITIES TO PROMOTE THE USE OF KNOWLEDGE AND SKILLS TO SOLVE PROBLEMS
Ask the children to:
• make notes to explain the reasons why the regions of Spain have retained their own identities.
• produce a poster, in groups, advertising different types of holidays in Spain.

ACTIVITIES TO ENCOURAGE ANALYTICAL THINKING

Ask the children to:

• compare and contrast life in Madrid or Barcelona with a city in the UK.

• use reference books and the Internet to research the work of Gaudí and review the importance of his work as an architect in Barcelona.

ACTIVITIES TO PROMOTE CREATIVITY

Ask the children to:

• look at pictures of Parc Guell in Barcelona and create their own mosaic using small pieces of coloured paper.

• research the work of Joan Miró (or Salvador Dali or Pablo Picasso) and create a picture in that style using a computer paint software package.

ACTIVITIES TO HELP CHILDREN USE EVIDENCE TO FORM OPINIONS AND EVALUATE CONSEQUENCES OF DECISIONS

Ask the children to:

• write a report, giving reasons, why it is important to protect Spain's national parks.

• work in pairs and decide on five items that would best represent life in Spain.

B: ACTIVITIES BASED ON DIFFERENT LEARNING STYLES

ACTIVITIES FOR LINGUISTIC LEARNERS

Ask the children to:

• write a rap to promote a Spanish Mediterranean coastal resort.

• write a report about why people visit Spain for their holidays, and the advantages and disadvantages for Spain having lots of tourists.

ACTIVITIES FOR LOGICAL AND MATHEMATICAL LEARNERS

Ask the children to:

• use reference books and the Internet to find out about the climate in the different regions of Spain and to show this information graphically.

ACTIVITIES FOR VISUAL LEARNERS

Ask the children to:

• select one place in Spain and design a visually appealing poster, with a slogan, that could be used to advertise it.

• locate the major cities and rivers on a map of Spain.

ACTIVITIES FOR KINAESTHETIC LEARNERS

Ask the children to:

• plan and help to make a Spanish family meal.

ACTIVITIES FOR MUSICAL LEARNERS

Ask the children to:

• dance the flamenco to some Spanish music.

• create a short radio advertisement and radio station jingle to advertise a place or tourist attraction in Spain.

ACTIVITIES FOR INTER-PERSONAL LEARNERS

Ask the children to:

• write a letter to a child living in Madrid, explaining their lifestyle (school, leisure pursuits, locality).

• plan an imaginary visit to Spain for their family.

ACTIVITIES FOR INTRA-PERSONAL LEARNERS

Ask the children to:

• describe what they imagine it would be like travelling on an AVE (high-speed tilting train) at up to 300km per hour between Seville and Madrid.

ACTIVITIES FOR NATURALISTIC LEARNERS

Ask the children to:

• prepare a speech for a debate on either the pros or cons of maintaining the national parks in Spain.

LINKS ACROSS THE CURRICULUM

The **Travel Through** series offers up-to-date information and cross-curricular opportunities for teaching geography, literacy, numeracy, history, RE, PSHE and citizenship.

The series enables children to develop an overview ('the big picture') of each country. This overview reflects the diversity and richness of the life and culture of each country. The series aims to prevent the development of misconceptions, stereotypes and prejudices, which often develop when the focus of a study narrows too quickly onto a small locality within a country. The books will help children not only to gain access to this overview, but also to develop an understanding of how places are connected. They contribute to the children's geographical knowledge, skills and understanding, and help them to make sense of the world around them.